An Eye on the Coast
The Fishing Industry from Wick to Whitby

D1610640

G.WILSON.

An Eye on the Coast
The Fishing Industry from Wick to Whitby

Gloria Wilson

TEMPUS

Frontispiece: *Galilee WY68* was built by W&G Stephen at Macduff in 1932 for Whitby owners.

First published 2006

Tempus Publishing Limited
The Mill, Brimscombe Port,
Stroud, Gloucestershire, GL5 2QG
www.tempus-publishing.com

© Gloria Wilson, 2006

The right of Gloria Wilson to be identified as the Author
of this work has been asserted in accordance with the
Copyrights, Designs and Patents Act 1988.

British Library Cataloguing in Publication Data.
A catalogue record for this book is available from the British Library.

ISBN 0 7524 3853 0

Typesetting and origination by Tempus Publishing Limited.
Printed in Great Britain.

Contents

Acknowledgements

I would like to thank all those kindly and supportive people who provided the information which has enabled me to put this book together. It is impossible to name them individually because there are so many of them.

My involvement with the fishing communities has been a rewarding and happy experience.

Sunset at North Shields *c.*1960. Note the two steam-powered trawlers in the distance. Situated near the mouth of the river Tyne the port was also a base for wooden cruiser-sterned diesel engined vessels of chiefly Scottish build.

Introduction

These photographs and drawings are a personal celebration of fisher people, harbours and boats along the coasts of Scotland and parts of north-east England. In no sense is the book a complete record of vessels and fishing communities and there are many gaps and omissions.

Inevitably there is an element of serendipity and chance. Some subjects were deliberately sought after during my work as a maritime writer and photographer, whereas others were taken fortuitously.

In particular I have selected the pictures for aesthetic appeal as well as for documentary content. Many of the images reflect my appreciation of the classic wooden-hulled, cruiser-sterned seine netters and dual-purpose craft which were among the most likeable and successful types of fishing boat built during the twentieth century.

But in wishing to give a broader view I have not neglected other vessel types. Introduced to the seiner trawler fleet in the 1960s the transom stern afforded more space aft above and below deck and quickly found favour.

From the early 1970s there was also a tremendous switch to steel vessels in the below 80ft section of the fleet. With one or two exceptions the majority of pictures show boats within the 30ft to 85ft size range. These were the craft I especially came to know and enjoy. Scores have perished under the heinous decommissioning schemes of recent years and my photographs could be viewed as a lament to a passing epoch.

But these splendid vessels did not exist in isolation. Shore-based activities were often pictorially vivid and harbours made enchanting settings.

Humour played a part. Some unusual and pleasing discoveries were made.

As a general code I have presented the photographs in the order in which I took them, except where perhaps a group of images work together more satisfactorily.

I hope the photographs and drawings bring much pleasure and evoke many memories.

Gloria Wilson, 2005.

Author's note

It is customary at the start of the second millennium to use metric measurements and weights but British equivalents are used in much of the book to avoid filling the captions with a rash of brackets and decimal points.

All but the newer boats were built to British dimensions, and other information in the book dates back to pre-metric days.

A few principal equivalents are given here:

1 inch = 25.400 millimetres.
1 foot (12in) = 304.800 millimetres.
1 cran (approx 3½cwt) = 177.800 kilograms.
1 mile = 1.6093 kilometres.

one

First Enthusiasms;

Points of Departure

My first enthusiasm was for the curiously shaped English square-sterned cobles which worked from beaches and tidal harbours in north-east England. Later I encountered Scottish ring-netters and drifters in Whitby during the last great Yorkshire herring fishings.

As a Durham student I discovered North Shields which, in the early 1960s, was the base for Scottish vessels working fly-dragging seine nets and nephrop trawls. There too I saw some of the last working steam-powered trawlers and herring drifters.

In the 1960s I made my first visits to Scotland. During the 1950s around a dozen Scottish boatyards had produced between them as many as fifty wooden-hulled cruiser-sterned boats each year.

The design techniques employed in the majority of these yards had long been based more on art, intuition and personal opinion than science but nevertheless this was a sound development of a series of boats which have proved themselves in rough seas over many years.

Basically the cruiser stern can be described as a sharp-ended counter which rakes forward at the centreline and has its fullest part at or below the waterline. Some argue that the cruiser stern is advantageous in a following sea and affords superior manoeuvrability particularly when working the fly-dragging seine net which in the early 1960s was the chief means of catching white fish in Scotland.

Dual purpose craft up to 75ft or so were built for herring drifting and great-lining in addition to seine net fishing.

In 1962 I enjoyed a short, breezy trip to sea with the Macduff seiner *Faithful Again BF267* which had just been built by John Watt & Sons at Banff. Three years later Watt acquired the Macduff Engineering Co. and became Macduff Boatbuilding & Engineering Co. Today the firm survives mightily as Macduff Shipyards, the most productive fishing boat builder in the United Kingdom.

Although it produces steel craft up to 90ft or so, it is the only UK shipyard to continue building timber-hulled fishing vessels up to 70ft long in the early years of the second millennium.

But in the 1960s I saw wooden boats under construction in maybe fifteen yards in Scotland and north-east England.

One Whitby builder, latterly known as Whitehall Shipyard, built a variety of types including Danish anchor seiners, Scottish-inspired ring-netters, dual-purpose boats and English cobles.

Summer in North Shields. Nephrop trawler *Radiant Star PD159* was built in 1956 by Gerrard Brothers at Arbroath for Peterhead owners. There was also still some herring fishing off the English north-east coast. *Wydale YH105* on the right was one of the last working steam drifters. Owned by Easticks of Yarmouth she was built of wood in 1917 at Lowestoft. North Shields early 1960s.

Mellow autumn light in 1961 in Eyemouth.

English fishermen fished from North Shields with Scottish-built boats. *Snowflake BF309* was constructed in 1948 by John Watt & Sons at Gardenstown shortly before the firm moved to Banff. North Shields, 1960s.

Seen here ashore for their annual overhaul, the cobles *Golden Crown WY78* and *Coronation Queen WY75* were built in 1953 for Staithes owners. J&J Harrison at Amble built *Coronation Queen* while *Golden Crown* came from William Clarkson (Whitby) Ltd. Staithes, late 1950s.

This 30ft coble went overseas. Named *Federal Star* she was ordered from William Clarkson for experimental fishing in Aden. Whitby, early 1961.

Whitehall Shipyard produced the Danish type anchor seiner *Ann's WY178* and the stalwart potter, long liner, herring drifter and fly-dragging seiner *Lead Us 11 A291* in the late 1940s and 1959 respectively. Whitby, *c.*1961.

Stardust LH228 (left) and *Achates LH232* were characteristic Scottish canoe-sterned herring ring netters built in 1947 at St Monans by Walter Reekie for the Musselburgh fleet. Whitby, *c.*1960.

Built at Whitehall Shipyard in 1957 *Whitby Rose WY110* was similar to a Scottish herring ring netter. Whitby, *c*.1961.

Success KY211 was constructed in 1960 by Smith & Hutton (Boatbuilders) Ltd at Anstruther for Whitby skipper, James Leadley. She was a characteristic, small, sturdy Scottish seine netter. Whitby, early 1960s.

Left and below: In 1963 Fraserburgh came second after Aberdeen for the weight of Scottish seine net landings. I saw many attractive cruiser-sterned seiners. *Fruitful Vine FR195* was built in 1957 by Thomas Summers & Co. in Fraserburgh. *Star Divine BF119* was constructed in 1958 by Summers and *Gamrie Bay BF141* in 1959 by John Watt & Sons at Banff. Fraserburgh, early 1960s.

In 1960 Summers produced the 32.7ft creel and small–line boat *Valiant FR231* and in 1961 the
53ft drifter–seiner *Quiet Waters FR253*.Sadly in 1962 the yard closed. Fraserburgh, early 1960s.

Measuring only 31ft the seiner *Primrose BF258* was constructed in 1961 by the Macduff Engineering Co. The 58ft *Monarch BF179* came from the same yard in 1959. Macduff, 1962.

I saw these sad remains in Buckpool, which lies to the west of Buckie's Cluny Harbour, in the early 1960s.

John Watt & Sons at Banff delivered the 54ft seiner *Faithful Again BF267* in 1962 to the Mitchell family of Macduff. Macduff, 1962.

Small, sturdy sweet-lined cruiser-sterned boats around 30ft long were known as yoles. About thirty came from Thomas Summers including the 31ft *Brilliant BF208* built in 1960 for owners in Portsoy. Whitehills, 1962.

Here Skipper Frank West's 75ft *Bdellium FR185* sets out from Fraserburgh in the early 1960s for a herring drifting trip. She was launched from Thomas Summers in 1960.

The 33ft 6in yole *Shamariah FR245* built by Summers in 1961 was still fishing from Fraserburgh some forty years later. Fraserburgh, 1972.

Above and below: During the 1960s the steam-powered herring drifter *Lizzie West LT495* was broken up. She was built by Herd & Mackenzie at Buckie in 1930 when some 800 steam drifters belonged to Scotland. Later sold to England she became one of the last steam drifters in service. Fraserburgh, 1960s.

Scottish motor drifters were colourful sights at the English herring fishings during the twenty years following the Second World War. *Faithful Star BF127* was constructed in 1958 by J&G Forbes & Co. at Sandhaven. *Lively Hope FR172* was built as an MFV by Walter Reekie at St Monans. Whitby, early 1960s.

The boat in the centre is the 60ft *Watchful BF107*. Completed in 1958, she was the final boat from Fraserburgh boat builders Wilson Noble & Co. which closed in 1959 after sixty years in business. Fraserburgh, early 1960s.

Above: MFVs, or 'motor fishing vessels', were constructed during the Second World War for various wartime tasks. Come peacetime, they were converted for fishing. The 75ft 7in Fraserburgh herring drifter *Spectrum FR76* was built by Humphrey & Smith at Grimsby. Whitby, early 1960s.

Right: Herring drifter *Tea Rose FR346* was delivered as MFV No.1217 from Wilson Noble. Fraserburgh, early 1960s.

Above: Produced as a seine netter by Smith & Hutton in 1961 for Portgordon near Buckie, the 55ft *Elma BCK139* later switched to white fish and nephrop trawling. Buckie, 1965.

Left: Fruitful Bough LK403 was built by J&G Forbes in the late 1930s as the herring drifter *Helen West BF363* for the West family of Gardenstown. Under subsequent owners she was fitted for seine netting. Aberdeen, 1965.

Right: Delivered from Jones Buckie Shipyard Ltd to Skipper Eric Smith in 1966, the 71ft 3in *Rhodella BCK110* was a typical eye-sweet cruiser-sterned seine net vessel. Aberdeen, *c.*1970.

Below: The 51ft seine netter and nephrop trawler *Guiding Star PD322* was built by the Macduff Engineering Co. in 1959 for Peterhead owners but later joined the Eyemouth fleet. Eyemouth, 1962.

Above: Built by Richard Irvin & Sons Ltd at Peterhead in 1954 the 73ft herring drifter and great-line vessel *Silver Hope FR29,* originally *PD377,* was sleek and elegant with a 19ft 6in beam and a Gardner 152hp engine. She later switched to trawling. Aberdeen, 1970.

Left: A notebook in Irvin's office gave a brief record of boats built by the firm. Of course, files containing detailed particulars were also kept. Designed as a drifter and great-liner *Honey Bee PD110* was built to the same lines as *Silver Hope* but was 1ft shorter.

Irvin produced the 76ft great-line boat *William Wilson 11 KY123* in 1956 for Skipper William Wilson. The lining grounds were prolific after the Second World War and halibut was plentiful. Great-line vessels often worked three-week trips to rocky ground around the Faroes, Rockall and Iceland. But the work involved tedious baiting and fish removal from hooks and by 1969 the method had almost died out. Aberdeen, 1960s.

Measuring 75ft long with a 20ft beam, *Utilise PD214* was built by Irvin in 1957 for the Duthie family. Here she sets out for a fly-dragging, seine-netting trip. Peterhead, 1960s.

Constructed by Irvin in 1960 for the Duncan family, *Fragrance PD345* became, in the 1970s, one of the last Scottish boats to work herring drift nets. Here she is equipped for fly-dragging seine net fishing. Aberdeen, 1960s.

The Baird family's 75ft by 20ft *Star of Peace PD324* was built in 1961 by Irvin. Skipper John Baird said 'Irvins made a bonnie model of a boatie'. Peterhead, 1960s.

Skipper Philip Morgan's 78ft 3in by 20ft 6in *Graceful PD343* was built by Irvin in 1961 to work seine nets off Norway and great-lines at Faroe and Rockall. Consequently she was built to a new design with fuller lines. Peterhead, 1972.

Left: Smith & Hutton built the 50ft *Ocean Herald KY39* in 1953 for Pittenweem which had developed as the chief seine net port in Fife. Pittenweem, 1960s.

Below: The same builder constructed the 55ft seiner *Altair LH418* in 1963 for Eyemouth. She was fitted with the new Gardner 6L3B 150hp engine to meet the demand for greater power.

two

Moving through
the 1970s

Years of Optimism

Fishermen moved into the 1970s against a background of great technical advances in the fishing industry. Fish was in high demand owing largely to a greater awareness of its nutritional importance.

The value of all species landed by UK vessels at Scottish ports rose from £22½ million in 1969 to £64 million in 1974.

Pair trawling for herring, and the further evolution of seine netting and trawling for white fish, called for powerful boats with greater sea range and catch-carrying capabilities.

Nets made from synthetic fibres yielded massive hauls. Gear handling efficiency was vastly improved by the use of hydraulically-powered winches, the power block and seine rope-storage reels.

Emphasis was placed on safety and catch quality with the introduction of gutting shelters and fish room chilling plants.

Electronic instruments became more effective and deckhouses became larger.

With changes in fishing methods and an increase in top weight, new cruiser-sterned vessels generally became fuller and beamier with deeper draught and more freeboard and deck space and greater buoyancy. Their bilges were harder and floors flatter and less hollow and they had larger propeller apertures.

During the 1970s there was a big demand for steel boats in the 70ft to 90ft size range. The material has advantages in terms of strength, and resistance to hard knocks from heavy fishing gear. By 1973 at least fifteen British yards were building steel vessels for Scottish owners.

Though the transom stern continued to find favour, many skippers chose the cruiser stern for both wooden and steel boats.

Some 400 new vessels, the majority in the 30ft to 80ft Registered Length range, joined the Scottish fleet in the years 1969 to 1974 inclusively. But many older craft continued to fish successfully and I photographed these gladly.

Despite the euphoria of much of the 1970s, there were sometimes economic woes and troubled times. Britain had entered the European Economic Community in 1973 and the Community extended its territorial waters to 200 miles. Politics became an issue. There were port blockades and protest marches.

But there were triumphs. Chief among these were developments at Peterhead. From being a failed herring port in the 1960s with weeds growing on the quaysides, it became by the close of the 1970s, the premier UK fishing port for the weight and value of all species of fish brought ashore.

A number of my photographs were taken in the light of the enthusiasm and 'oomph' which characterised Peterhead from 1970 onwards.

Earlier boats from Richard Irvin & Sons look lean and spare when compared with the buxom 78ft by 22ft seiners and herring pair trawlers *Achilles PD178* and *Ugievale 11 PD105*, built by the firm in the late 1960s for Skippers Andrew Strachan and Arthur Buchan. Peterhead, early 1970s.

Left and below: Forthright KY173 and *Steadfast KY170*, produced by Irvin in 1969 for Skippers Robert and Alec Gardner, were even heftier forward than *Achilles* and *Ugievale 11.* Aberdeen and Peterhead respectively, *c.*1970.

Skipper John C Buchan's 79ft and 495hp seiner and herring pair trawler *Sparkling Star PD108* came from Irvin in 1970 but had finer lines than *Achilles, Ugievale 11, Forthright* and *Steadfast*. Peterhead, 1972.

Irvin delivered the 79ft seiner trawler *Starcrest PD114* in 1971 to Skipper George Collin. Her Caterpillar 565hp engine gave her good towing power for herring pair trawling. Peterhead, 1971.

Measuring 74.4ft with 20ft 3in beam, *Stanhope 11 PD115* was slighter in shape and construction than the full-bodied 78-footers from Irvin. She was built in 1968 for Skipper Peter Strachan. Peterhead, 1973.

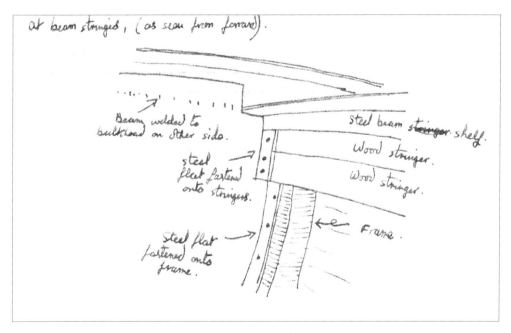

When *Stanhope 11* was being built, I made some rough sketches showing her internal construction. Peterhead, 1968.

Delivered from Irvin in 1971 to Skipper John W Addison, the 79ft by 22ft 6in seiner trawler *Reliant BCK36* sets out for her sea trials. Peterhead, 1971.

Skipper Andrew Reid's 80ft seiner trawler *Ulysses PD76* was built in 1972 by Irvin. Unlike other Scottish yards Irvin never did build a transom-sterned fishing boat. Peterhead, 1972.

In 1970 seine net skippers boycotted Aberdeen in protest against high charges for landing fish at the port. The majority went to Peterhead where catches were laid out for auction in the open air upon any available quay space. Peterhead, 1970.

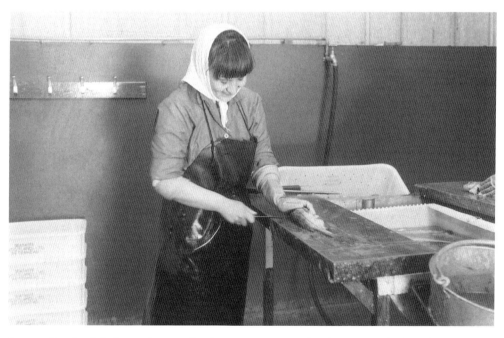

Seataste (Scotland) Ltd went into production in 1972 at Peterhead to process high quality seine net fish. It bought chiefly cod and haddock which was filleted by hand. Some ninety-five per cent was exported to North America. Peterhead, 1972.

The Fairmile Construction Co. built the 79ft 9in steel seiner trawler *Fairweather IV PD107* at Berwick upon Tweed in 1969 for Skipper John Alec Buchan. She worked in the group of Peterhead herring pair trawlers known as the 'Big Five'. Peterhead, 1969.

J&G Forbes delivered the 77ft by 22ft 6in seiner trawler *Fruitful Bough PD109* in 1970 to Skipper William Buchan. She had a Caterpillar 450hp motor. Peterhead, 1970s.

The inshore fishermen continued their boycott of Aberdeen. *Fairweather 1V* is seen here passing through the lifting bridge into the North Harbour at Peterhead. The pitch-roofed building on the right was the newly opened Greenhill fish market. Later the North Harbour was deepened and reshaped and the fish market vastly extended. Peterhead, 1971.

Opposite: This group of seiner trawlers illustrates the different vessel types fishing from Peterhead in the mid 1970s. In the foreground are two wooden-hulled boats, one with transom stern and the other with cruiser stern. The middle two are steel. The one with the light-coloured hull is the transom-sterned *Morning Dawn PD195* built by John R Hepworth on Humberside in 1975 for Skipper David Morgan. In the distance is another cruiser-sterned boat with wooden hull. Peterhead, 1975.

Delivered from J&G Forbes in 1970, Skipper James Slater's transom-sterned herring trawler *Aquarius FR55* ran her trials in a snowstorm. Fraserburgh, 1970.

Skipper James Slater, behind on the right, with crewmembers on board *Aquarius*. Fraserburgh, 1970.

Fellowship FR400 was built in 1952 as *Star O'Buchan FR309* by Thomas Summers. Sold to New Zealand in 1977 she was still there in 2001 working as a long liner. Fraserburgh, 1972.

With a lack of seriousness the ship painter lettered the New Zealand port name upside down before *Fellowship* left Scotland. Fraserburgh, 1977.

The 73ft white fish, herring and sprat trawler *Hawthorn FR25* (centre) was built by Summers in 1953 as the seiner drifter *Ritchies FR25* and had a Gardner 152hp engine. This was later replaced by a Kelvin 320hp unit. *Rambler FR5* (right) could be classed as a motor half-zulu with her stern less raked than that of a classic sailing zulu. Fraserburgh white fish market, 1972.

Opposite above: Skipper Donald McIver's stalwart 61ft by 20ft nephrop trawler *Olive Branch SY95* was launched in 1971 from J&G Forbes. Fittings included a Gardner 230hp engine. Her topsides were planked with iroko, a hard and durable West African timber. Boats built by Forbes were launched ready to go to sea under their own power to nearby Fraserburgh for completion.

Opposite below: Silver Bell INS52, constructed in 1971, and *Silver Gem INS61,* completed in 1972, were herring pair trawling and ring-netting partners and had Gardner 230hp engines. James Noble (Fraserburgh) Ltd built them for Skippers David Patience and William McLeman Jack from Avoch. Noble had built many ring netters but these later ones were designed to suit changing fishing patterns with more powerful motors and heavier deck machinery. Nevertheless, they had graceful ring-netter lines. Fraserburgh, 1972.

Measuring 70ft by 20ft *Day Dawn FR66* was built by Jones Buckie Shipyard in 1960 as *Stanhope PD335* for Peterhead skipper, Peter Strachan. Off Aberdeen, 1970.

Opposite above: These name boards were fastened to a shed within the premises of ship's carpenters Buchan, Hall & Mitchell. Fraserburgh, 1971.

Opposite below: The 86ft round bilge transom-sterned 600hp Spinningdale class steel pocket trawler *Jasirene A373* was launched in 1972 from John Lewis & Sons Ltd in Aberdeen for Skipper James Duncan and the John Wood Group. Aberdeen, 1972.

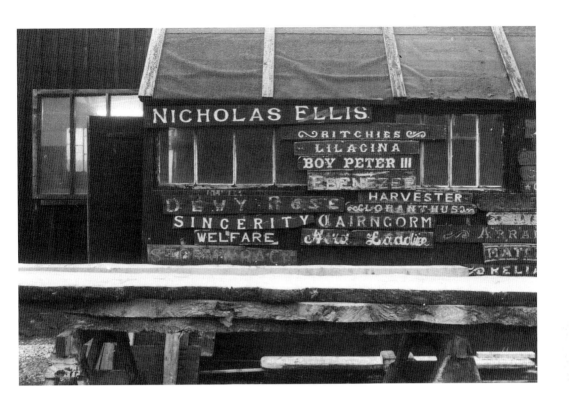

Sundari PD93, built by Lewis in 1972 for Peterhead skipper William Morgan was a seiner trawler version of the Spinningdale class vessels. She had a Mirrlees Blackstone 600hp engine. Peterhead, 1977.

Opposite above: At the start of the 1970s Aberdeen was Scotland's top fishing port and the home for a hundred deep sea trawlers. Here two traditional 'side-winders' set out for the grounds. Off Aberdeen, 1972.

Opposite below: Hall, Russell & Co. in Aberdeen built the 113ft motor trawler *Aberdeen Distributor A211* in 1957 when many trawler owners were disposing of their elderly and decrepit steam-powered vessels. Aberdeen, 1972.

Built by Macduff Boatbuilding & Engineering Co. in 1973 for Skipper John Scott, the 56ft transom-sterned seiner trawler *Aurelia BF176* had a Caterpillar 300hp motor. Trials day, Macduff, 1973.

Herd & Mackenzie at Buckie built the 71.3ft seiner trawler *Minerva BCK24* in 1970 for Skipper Alex McKay. At this time seiners landed about half the total Scottish white fish catch. Peterhead, 1974.

Macduff Boatbuilding delivered the 65ft seiner *Dioscuri BF151* in 1972 to Skipper John Mitchell. Peterhead, 1974.

Prowess BF460, built by Macduff Boatbulding in 1967 for Skipper George West, was one of the first herring purse seiners to join the Scottish fleet. Fraserburgh, 1974.

During the early 1970s Skipper David Smith's 78ft seiner *Argonaut 111 KY337* became the first boat in Scotland to fit seine rope-storage reels and a gutting shelter. These later became standard equipment in the seine net fleet. *Argonaut 111* came in 1969 from Jones Buckie Shipyard. Aberdeen, 1975.

Rope reels on-board *Argonaut 111*. These reels eliminated the dangerous manual tasks of arranging coils of rope on deck when the gear was being hauled, and later standing near them to ensure that they ran out again smoothly. Aberdeen, 1974.

Skipper John H. Mackay's 60ft seiner *Delightful BF121* was constructed in 1958 by Jones
Buckie Shipyard and had a Gardner 114hp engine. Aberdeen, 1970.

Jones Buckie also owned a yard at Lossiemouth where in 1975 it built the 54ft transom
sterned seiner trawler *Derona A242* for Skipper Albert McIntosh and the Don Fishing Co.
Aberdeen, 1970s.

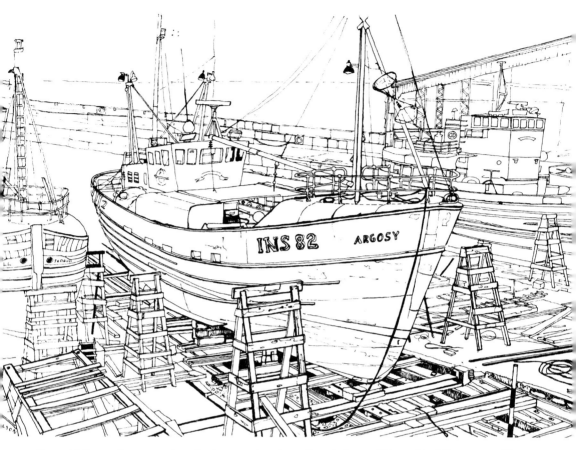

Round bilge cruiser-sterned steel seiner trawlers from Campbeltown Shipyard had lines not unlike those of wooden vessels. Measuring 79ft 11in long with 22ft beam, *Argosy INS82* was built as *Ajax* in 1972 for Skipper William Campbell and was powered by a Caterpillar 480hp engine.

Skipper Campbell believed in the superiority of Scottish cruiser-sterned boats from the point of view of seaworthiness and gear-handling capabilities. Buckie, 1970s.

Opposite above: Cavalier INS109 was produced by Campbeltown Shipyard in 1973 for Skipper James McPherson. Peterhead, 1975.

Opposite below: Skipper James Campbell fished with the seiner trawler *Andromeda INS167* delivered in 1975 from Campbeltown Shipyard. She was the tenth boat built to the Campbeltown 80 design. Peterhead, 1981.

Peterhead's new fish market at Greenhill could accommodate 7,000 boxes of fish. Peterhead, mid-1970s.

Opposite above: The 80ft seiner trawler *Replenish FR199* handed over to Skipper James Green in 1975 was the hundredth vessel built by Richard Irvin. Founded in 1914 the yard initially built steam drifters and in 1937 produced its first cruiser-sterned motor boat. Peterhead, 1975.

Opposite below: In the mid-1970s about 350 boats landed white fish at Peterhead. *Radiant Star FR127* was built by J&G Forbes in 1973 for Skipper Alex Wiseman. Peterhead, 1975.

The 85ft by 24ft seiner trawler *Sunbeam INS189* constructed in 1978 for Skipper William Smith was the largest and final vessel from Richard Irvin. Peterhead *c*.1979.

Above and opposite below: On Monday 31 March 1975 eighty boats blockaded Aberdeen as part of the fishermen's protest against the political and economic situation. In all, some 870 vessels blocked Scottish ports. The fishermen were angered by low priced imports of fish and also wanted Britain's territorial waters to be extended.

This page and opposite above: More than 700 members of the Scottish fishing industry marched through Aberdeen in June 1977 to demonstrate for a 50-mile exclusive territorial zone for British fishermen. The European fisheries commissioner was visiting Scotland but he said that a tight and well-controlled quota system was the answer to conservation.

Skipper Tommy Milne's seiner *Starella PD112* was crippled by a huge rope which wrapped itself round her propeller. She is seen here on the slipway with the rope in the foreground. Peterhead, 1975.

Above and below: CoSalt was set up in 1873 under the splendid name The Great Grimsby Coal, Salt and Tanning Co. Ltd. Among its many chandlery services it developed a twine and net-making division of worldwide significance.

In 1973 former skipper Peter Buchan worked at the Fraserburgh net factory and Margaret Hamilton at the Granton factory.

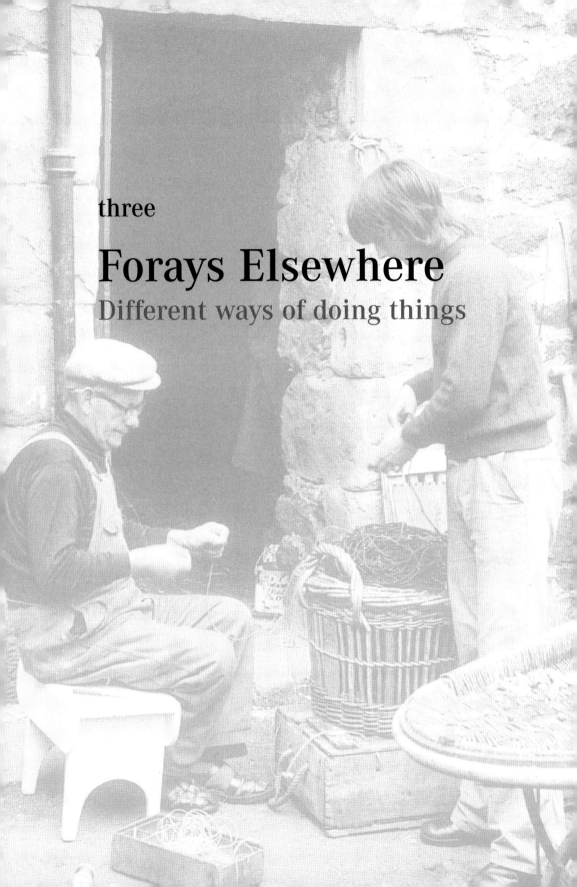

three

Forays Elsewhere

Different ways of doing things

Much of my time was spent along the Scottish north-east coast but I made forays elsewhere.

All fisher towns and villages have their individual character and ways of doing things. Some of my photographs from the 1970s show a state of affairs which seems aeons away from that of today. Set into cliffs the fishing village of Gourdon was strong in tradition. Fishermen wore blue ganseys, lines were baited in charming back yards and Arbroath owned some of the oldest boats still fishing full-time in British waters.

Rather than building large efficient vessels which could work further afield and catch more fish, many fishermen were content to make a modest living from local grounds in these elderly boats which were economical to run.

Many good quality cruiser-sterned boats from the 1950s and '60s also continued working from Scottish and English ports.

Some fishing communities occupied singular geographical settings. Hartlepool in north-east England lies near the mouth of the river Tees in the centre of one of Britain's most heavily industrialised areas.

Even so, Peterhead and Fraserburgh continued to provide rewarding subjects. My photographs on pages 84 and 85, showing boats in Fraserburgh, are full of information and illustrate transitions in design. All but *Achilles PD178* were built by J&G Forbes. Measuring 73ft by 20ft, *Harvest Hope FR120* was delivered in 1960 as *Dayspring FR120* and was one of a series of cruiser-sterned boats designed primarily as seiners, drifters and great-liners.

Of similar type the 75ft by 20ft *Shepherd Lad FR215* was constructed in 1958 as *Animation PD279* and both she and *Dayspring* had Gardner 152hp engines.

Built with pair trawling in mind the remaining three had fuller lines and greater power. Delivered in 1969 the 68ft by 20ft *Surveillance BF11* was powered by a Caterpillar 270hp motor. Note her plump cruiser stern.

At 75ft with 21ft beam, the transom-sterned *Atlantic Star PD177* was built in 1973 and fitted with a robust Grenaa 550hp, 500rpm engine which turned the variable pitch propeller by direct drive.

The full-bodied *Achilles* (see above photo on page 33) had a Caterpillar 375hp engine.

In 1976 some forty boats took part in the sprat fishing.

English square-sterned cobles built by J&J Harrison at Amble in Northumberland were celebrated for their superb and elegant lines.

Emulate, Treasure and *Honour,* (left to right), fished with salmon drift or beach nets.
Larger cobles including the 34ft *Provider* could work salmon drift nets and crab and lobster pots.
Amble, 1969.

For many years Gourdon was one of the few Scottish ports from which small lining was carried out to any extent. In 1972 about a dozen boats were lining for high quality cod and haddock. Gourdon, 1972.

Sometimes fish was more plentiful on the seine netting grounds. Note the seine net ropes aboard these boats. Gourdon, early 1970s.

This appealing little vessel the 36ft *Enterprise ME155* worked lines and creels in 1975 from Gourdon under Skipper Alexander Welsh Jnr. Built by Walter Reekie at St Monans in 1931 she was one of the earliest canoe-sterned fishing boats. Gourdon, 1975.

Alexander Welsh Snr (left) skippered *Enterprise* until handing her over to his son. Here lines are sorted. Gourdon, 1975.

In 1975 Skipper Steven Morrison's *Quest 111 ME61* trawled for haddock and flatfish. She was built in 1950 as the seiner and ring-netter *Hope KY136* by James N. Miller & Sons at St Monans. Gourdon, 1975.

A catch comes ashore from Skipper Robert Paton's 50ft *Day Dawn ME101* which in late spring 1981 was one of two seiners working from Gourdon. Other boats fished with trawls. Gourdon, 1981.

Above: During the late spring 1981 only the forty-nine-year-old *Silver Quest ME150* (left) fished with lines from Gourdon. About four boats including *Enterprise* (right) worked crab and lobster creels. Gourdon, 1981.

Left: In 1981 Skipper Alan Donaldson's 47ft *Concord ME126* also worked light trawls from Gourdon. Originally *LH416* she was built in 1965 by Weatherhead & Blackie at Port Seton. Gourdon, 1981.

Opposite: On one occasion in 1981 *Concord* put ashore an exceptionally large catch which comprised forty boxes of cod, one box of lemon soles, one large monkfish, a ling and a pollack, all caught in some twelve hours. Gourdon, 1981.

In 1973 North Shields was the fifth highest earning English port after Hull, Grimsby, Fleetwood and Lowestoft. Its geographical position at the mouth of the river Tyne in relation to both sea and land gave it huge potential and the growing industrial area of Tyneside provided an increasing demand for fish.

White fish catches came mainly from seiners and trawlers under 80ft long including many Scots.

Right: A recent addition to the North Shields fleet was the seiner *Celerity LK187*. Built in 1933 she was the first cruiser-sterned boat from Herd & Mackenzie at Buckie. North Shields, 1973.

Below: Local skipper, Norman Morse, trawled for white fish with the 66ft cruiser-sterned *Conmoran BCK92* which was built in 1959 at Jones Buckie Shipyard. North Shields, 1973.

Some twenty boats at Hartlepool in the 1970s enjoyed keen demand for locally caught cod, haddock and whiting and also nephrops, crabs and lobsters.

Skipper Victor Deer fished up to 100 miles from port with the Danish-built anchor seiner *David Helen HL6*. Hartlepool, 1973.

Opposite above and below: Several fishermen worked second-hand Scottish vessels from Hartlepool. Skipper Peter Watt used fly-dragging seine nets with the 56ft *Press On BF65* (top) produced in 1956 by John Watt & Sons at Banff. The 60ft fly-dragging seiner *Acacia BF199* (below) was built in 1960 by James Noble (Fraserburgh) Ltd. Hartlepool, 1973.

Canoe-sterned ring-netters had very pretty lines. Alexander Noble & Sons at Girvan produced the 56ft ringer, seiner and nephrop trawler *Silver Quest BA302* in 1967 for owners in Dunure. Girvan, 1975.

Opposite above: In 1975 Alexander Noble delivered the 69ft seiner trawler *Wanderer 11 BA76* to David and Kenneth Gibson. She was the fifth boat built by Noble for the Gibson family. Ayr, 1976.

Opposite below: The Gourdon 40ft light trawler *Morning Star ME106* was built by Alexander Noble in 1950 as *Girl Maureen BA128*. Gourdon, 1981.

Bruce's AH94 was built by James N Miller & Sons in 1927 as the motor fifie *Celtic KY171* and later sold to the Bruce family of Arbroath. Arbroath, 1975.

Skipper Sidney Cargill fished from Arbroath with the 55ft canoe-sterned *Girl Jean AH76* built in the 1940s at Anstruther by Walter Reekie. Arbroath, 1975.

Fortuna AH153 was constructed in 1890 as the sailing fifie *Isabella*. In the 1970s she worked creels under Skipper James Smith and had a Kelvin 66hp motor. Arbroath, 1975.

Skipper James Kidd trawled from Arbroath with the 53ft *Floresco AH72*. She was a product of Gerrard Brothers at Arbroath in 1959 and was powered by a Gardner 114hp engine. Arbroath, 1980.

Port Seton in 1980 commemorated the hundredth anniversary of the opening of its harbour. Many of the port's fleet of thirty two boats were at home to mark the event. Port Seton, 1980.

At the start of the 1980s Pittenweem supported around fifty seiners and white fish and nephrop trawlers. Here are some of them in soft and shimmering sunlight. Pittenweem, early 1980s.

Above and below: R. R. Spink & Sons produced tasty succulent Arbroath smokies in the traditional manner. Fresh small haddock were headed, cleaned and dry-salted and hung in pairs over racks. They were smoked in a smoke-barrel kiln over a slow-burning hardwood fire. Arbroath, 1980.

Before the Second World War, Lossiemouth was the top Scottish seine net port but by 1975 it was struggling to survive. Less than twenty seiners landed catches there, including Skipper James Smith's 62ft 6in *Shannon 1V INS307*, built as *Covesea INS307* in 1965 by Herd and Mackenzie. Lossiemouth, 1975.

Plymouth skipper, Fred Ivey worked fly-dragging seine nets with the 63ft 6in *Atlantis PH67*. She was built as *INS73* for Lossiemouth in 1956 by Jones Buckie Shipyard. Plymouth, 1976.

Completed in 1959 the 73ft *Morann BCK114* was one of twenty-eight cruiser-sterned vessels built in the 1950s by Jones Buckie Shipyard. During the late 1970s she fished for nephrops and white fish under Skipper Joseph Murray. Buckie, 1975.

Surveillance BF11 (right) and *Harvest Hope FR120* had also fished exceedingly well.
Fraserburgh, 20 February 1976.

Opposite above: Early in 1976 huge shoals of sprats were located from the Moray Firth to Arbroath.
Pair trawlers *Achilles PD178* (right) and *Atlantic Star PD177* had fished mightily off
Collieston. *Achilles*'s echo sounder indicated a shoal four miles long.

Opposite below: Pair trawler *Shepherd Lad FR215* puts ashore large, good quality sprats caught four
to five miles offshore between Montrose and Arbroath.

Above: Under Skipper Donald Anderson *Glenugie 111 PD347* became in 1966, the first Scottish vessel to purse seine for herring. Later she returned to fly-dragging seining for white fish and was fitted with rope reels and gutting shelter. *Glenugie 111* was built in 1964 by Richard Irvin. Peterhead, 1976.

Right: Skipper Anderson is seen here alongside his later vessel, the 86ft steel hulled *Glenugie 1V PD340* delivered in 1980 from McTay Marine Ltd on Merseyside. She had separate decks for trawling and fly-dragging seining. Peterhead, 1980.

Opposite: Skipper Stanley Morgan's Norwegian-built steel trawler *Summer Dawn PD64* takes aboard a single-boat mid-water trawl in readiness for the English winter sprat fishery. Peterhead, 1977.

These seiners in Wick were (left to right), *Superb WK432, Valhalla WK171* and *Ardent WK55.* Skipper John Malcolm's *Ardent* was the oldest, built in the 1930s by Walter Reekie as the ring-netter *Ardent INS326* for Hopeman owners. Wick, 1977.

Opposite above: Built at Fraserburgh in 1955 *Daystar WK84* (left) fished from Wick under Skipper William Smith. Skipper Donald Plowman's *Morning Star WK27* was constructed by James N. Miller a year earlier. Wick 1977.

Opposite below: Skipper Hugh Calder's 70ft by 20ft 4in *Rosemary WK412* was built by Herd & Mackenzie in 1960 as *INS116* for Lossiemouth. Wick, 1977.

About two thirds of the Buckie fleet in the mid 1970s undertook light trawling for nephrops and white fish. Measuring 72ft with 19ft 6in beam, *Hall-Mark BCK121* was built in 1960 by Jones Buckie Shipyard. Buckie, 1978.

Built in 1964 by Herd & Mackenzie for Skipper William Herd the 74ft 4½in *Ardelle BCK227* was among the first below-80ft Scottish vessels specifically designed for white fish and herring trawling. Peterhead, 1977.

Skipper William Bain trawled for nephrops and white fish with the 53ft *Pilot Star BCK155*, built in 1964 by John Watt & Sons at Banff. Buckie, 1979.

Banff boatbuilders John Wyatt & Sons, who took over the Macduff Engineering Co. in the mid-1960s, built the 53ft 6in *Ben Arkle BF447* in 1967 for Skipper George Addison. Macduff 1979.

Above and below: More name boards in Fraserburgh in 1981.

Measuring 53ft, *The Way PD268* was built at Banff as *FR292* in 1965 by John Watt & Sons.
Peterhead, 1979.

Built by George Thomson & Son at Buckie in 1947, the 57ft *Braes O' Strathlene BCK175* trawled for sprats, nephrops and white fish in the late 1970s under Skipper Andrew Garden. Buckie, 1979.

Built in 1966 by the Ramsey Shipbulding & Engineering Co. in the Isle of Man, the 53ft 7in light trawler *Smallwood BCK27* fished out of Aberdeen. Fraserburgh, 1979.

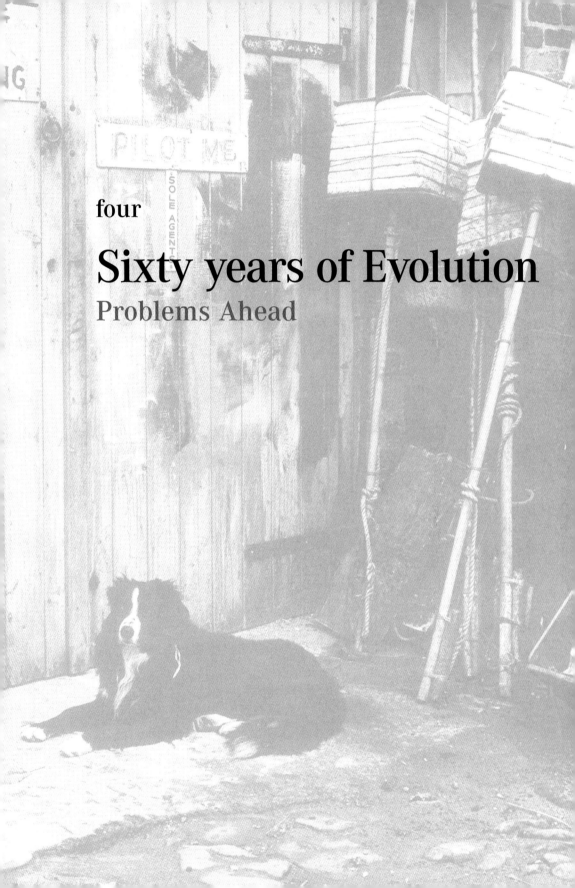

four

Sixty years of Evolution

Problems Ahead

My final selection of pictures could be viewed even more predominantly as a scrapbook, a visual diary or commonplace book.

It covers about twenty-eight years from 1976 to 2003 but with gaps in the narrative. Nevertheless, the boat illustrations represent sixty-six years of evolution in the medium-sized class of vessel from the cruiser-sterned seiner *Windsor FR280* built in 1934 to the single-net and twin-rig trawlers *Arcturus LK59* and *Our Lass WY797* completed in 2000.

Latterly twin-rig trawling, in which spread of the gear is more important than height, became increasingly important. Two nets are towed side by side in order to catch nephrops and quality groundfish.

Skippers chose compact twin-riggers with good towing capabilities resulting in economical running costs, and yet large enough to work offshore and withstand harsh weather.

Owned by Lockers Trawlers, *Our Lass* and her sister-ship *Rebecca WY790* were designed by Scottish naval architects S. C. McAllister & Co. to their owners' requirements and were built by Parkol Marine Engineering in Whitby. With round bilges and transom stern they measure 59ft 11in overall and draw 12ft 6in aft. Their massive 23ft beam made them two of the most spacious 60-footers yet built. Their shape and propulsion characteristics enable them to pull heavy, robust gear over rocky ground and also to grip the water and keep the net in position. In the interests of good towing qualities the fine entry provides a good flow of water to the propeller, housed in a nozzle. The semi-bulbous bow gives a longer keel length to improve directional stability and towing efficiency.

Both boats were built from ready-cut steel components supplied in kit form from Steel-Kit (UK) Ltd.

In the first few years of the second millennium, things have been tough, particularly for the white fish fleet. Scientists reported that cod stocks were near to collapse.

In May 2003 the European Union announced the framework for its five-to-ten-year North Sea cod recovery proposals. These centred on tight catch quotas and limits on the number of days boats may spend at sea.

Fishermen want a sustainable fishery. Their livelihood and future depends on it but many dislike the quota system because in a mixed fishery, it is impossible to catch specific species to order and it results in dead prime fish being dumped at sea.

In place of quotas many prefer conservation measures based predominantly on days at sea limits and the use of fishing gear designed to reduce the capture of unwanted species.

Skippers began to see signs that stocks were beginning to recover, resulting from net mesh size increases and vessel decommissioning schemes.

Generally some confidence in the future of the fishing industry has begun to return. Some new boats are being built, with the emphasis on safety, minimal operating costs and much greater catch quality. Numerous initiatives are also in hand ashore to maintain the quality of fish during marketing and processing.

In 2001 the Scottish fleet contained 950 vessels over 10m long compared with 1,362 ten years earlier. At the close of 2003 about 165 more boats had been decommissioned.

The decommissioning programmes have annihilated many beautiful fishing craft.

Among those illustrated in this book, *Snowflake*, *Watchful*, *Forthright*, *Enterprise*, *Sarepta*, *Strachans*, *Avoca, Moray Endurance* and others have been destroyed.

Though a smaller fleet leaves large areas of sea unfished, fishermen deplore destruction of the vessels and would prefer that they be found some other useful role.

Crystal Sea BF218 runs home during a breeze. The transom-sterned boat was built by Macduff Boatbuilding in 1974 for Skipper Albert Watt and was powered by a Kelvin 500hp engine. Macduff, 1978.

Crewmen mend a white fish bobbin trawl on-board Skipper Maurice Slater's *Star Award BF236*. There was a nice little revival in haddock, cod and whiting stocks in the Moray Firth.

Bobbin trawling for white fish was introduced to Macduff in the late 1960s to enable boats to work rougher ground than with the seine net. Built by Macduff Boatbuilding in 1975 the 56ft *Star Award* had a Caterpillar 360hp motor and a propeller nozzle to give her good towing capabilities for trawling. Macduff, 1977.

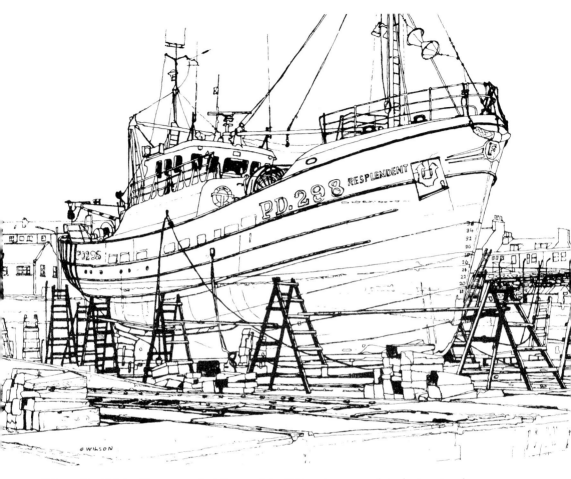

Skipper David John Forman took delivery of the 85ft cruiser-sterned steel seiner trawler *Resplendent PD298* in 1979 from Campbeltown Shipyard. Peterhead, 1981.

Opposite above: Measuring only 33ft long, *Gracious FR167* was another attractive little yole built in the 1950s by Thomas Summers & Co. Peterhead, 1981.

Opposite below: Frigate BCK26 was built as a seiner drifter in 1955 by Smith & Hutton. Here she is seen as *BA138* after being sold to Ayrshire owners. Later she was renamed *Jacana*. Ayr, 1976.

J&G Forbes handed over the 74ft transom-sterned white fish trawler *Altaire LK292* in 1978 to a partnership of seven Shetlanders headed by Skipper John Peter Duncan.

Skipper Duncan (right), and Mate Alistair Inkster. Fraserburgh, 1978.

Herd & Mackenzie's first transom-sterned wooden-hulled boat was the 55.85ft by 18.55ft seiner trawler *Seagull BF74* built in 1971 for Skipper Kenneth West. Macduff, 1977.

As the 1970s progressed, more boats were built with transom sterns rather than with cruiser sterns. The 70ft seiner trawler *Sharon Rose 11 LH317* was delivered from Macduff Boatbuilding in 1977 to George Moodie & Sons of Port Seton. Macduff, 1977.

Mackay Boatbuilders at Arbroath built the 61ft seiner trawler *Argus AH30* in 1971 for the four Teviotdale brothers. Arbroath, 1980.

Built by Mackay in 1976 for Skipper James Robb the 56ft and 280hp seiner trawler *Sparkling Star LK204* was the first new boat to join the Scalloway fleet for ten years. Sea trials, Arbroath 1976.

Skipper William Lawson fished with the 56ft transom-sterned white fish trawler *Rosebay PD313* built in 1979 by James Noble (Fraserburgh) Ltd. She bore the same name as a steam drifter which belonged to Skipper Lawson's grandfather. Peterhead, 1981.

At the start of the 1980s three-quarter-length shelter decks were becoming popular. Skipper John Coull's 75ft seiner trawler *Altair BCK266* was built in 1980 by Macduff Boatbuilding. The top of the shelter was shaped to harmonise with the lines of her hull. Peterhead, 1981.

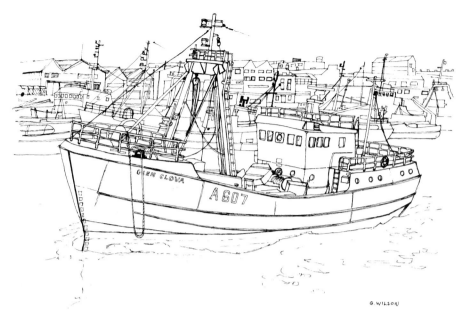

G. WILSON

The 90ft pocket trawler *Glen Clova A607* was built beside the river Thames by Cubow Ltd of London in 1976 for J. Marr (Aberdeen) Ltd and was powered by a B&W Alpha 700hp motor. She fished under Skipper Kenneth Walker. At this time about twenty-four vessels known as pocket trawlers fished from Aberdeen. They were economical successors to the larger traditional trawlers and were designed to make trips of up to ten days to the west of the Orkney and Shetland islands. Aberdeen, 1976.

The 53ft *Suilven BF290* was built in 1963 at Banff by John Watt & Sons as *Scottish Maid BF290*. Buckie, 1979.

Originally named *Marwood BA339,* the 39.80ft 120hp light trawler *Brighter Hope PD113* was produced in 1967 by James Noble (Fraserburgh) Ltd. Peterhead, 1979.

Constructed in 1959 *Craighall A322* was one of a number of 73ft cruiser-sterned steel seiner trawlers built by the Fairmile Construction Co. at Berwick. These vessels were known as 'sputniks' after the launch in 1957 of the Sputnik space satellite. Later *Craighall* was equipped for scallop fishing. Buckie, 1980.

Seiner trawler *Lothian Rose LH38* was delivered in 1970 to Skipper Robert Clark of Musselburgh from Jones Buckie Shipyard. Built from lines designed by G. L. Watson & Co. she had a Caterpillar 450hp motor. Peterhead, 1978.

There was a big move towards white fish pair trawling by the Peterhead–based fleet in the 1970s. Here Skipper Arthur Buchan's 87ft steel trawler *Lorenzo FD348* takes aboard a pair trawl for towing over rocky ground. Peterhead, 1978.

Right: Completed in 1981 Skipper Albert Ritchie's chunky 75ft by 23ft transom-sterned herring and white fish trawler *Quiet Waters 111 FR353* is seen here under construction at Macduff Boatbuilding. Macduff, 1980.

Below: A purse seine comes ashore from the 138ft *Kings Cross FR381,* a second-hand Norwegian-built vessel bought by Skipper Alec Masson. In 1978 Scotland owned thirty-six pursers. Fraserburgh, 1979.

Herd & Mackenzie built the 56ft yellow-hulled seiner trawler *Flourish LK450* in 1980 for Skipper Joseph Kay and a group of Shetland fishermen. Shooting rollers on the Fishing Hydraulics seine rope reels enabled ropes to be run off above head level. *Flourish* measured below 25tons under Scottish Part IV Registry and had a Volvo 290hp motor with 5.16:1 reduction gear. Buckie, trials day, 1980.

I remember *Golden Sceptre BF152* at the Yorkshire herring drifting. Built by J&G Forbes in 1959 for Skipper Alec West she later switched to trawling. Peterhead, 1980.

In 1981 Herd & Mackenzie built its final cruiser-sterned boat. The 75ft seiner trawler *Avoca BCK294* was owned by the Fishermen's Mutual Association (Buckie) Ltd and leased to Skipper David Campbell. Buckie, 1981.

Above: Some of the earliest cruiser-sterned boats were still fishing in the 1980s including the 52ft motor seiner *Windsor FR280* built in 1934 by J&G Forbes. Fraserburgh, 1980s.

Left: Net mending. Fraserburgh, 1980s.

Opposite:

Above: One of the largest, most powerful wooden-hulled herring pair trawlers was the 86ft 850hp *Sarepta FR207* handed over from J&G Forbes in 1976 to Skipper John Noble. Peterhead, 1980.

Below: Only four or five great-line boats worked from Aberdeen in 1981, including the 83ft *Strachan's FR197* delivered from J&G Forbes in 1956 to the Strachan family. Aberdeen, 1981.

La Morlaye LH207 was produced in 1940 by George Forbes & Co. (Peterhead) Ltd as a seiner drifter. Peterhead, 1981.

Evening Star LK87, built by Macduff Boatbuilding in 1981 for Skipper David Smith of Scalloway was one of only a few wooden-hulled cruiser-sterned boats to be constructed in the 1980s. Macduff, 1981.

Seiner trawler *Moray Endurance BCK34*, delivered in 1986 from George Thomson & Son, was among the last wooden-hulled boats built in Scotland to have a cruiser stern. She fished under Skipper Tommy Ritchie. Peterhead, *c*.1990.

Built by Macduff Boatbulding in 1986 for Skipper Iain Philip, the hefty 75.72ft by 23ft seiner trawler *Tyleana BF61* was the final cruiser-sterned wooden-hulled boat to come from a Scottish yard. Peterhead. *c*.1990.

Skipper Tom Bain worked white fish pair trawls with the 71ft transom-sterned *Bonaventure LH111* built in 1987 by Herd & Mackenzie. She was a new design from 'Herdie's', with her stout 22ft beam extended for much of her length. Sea trials, Buckie, 1987.

Fishing under Skipper James Buchan, the 80ft steel-hulled cruiser-sterned seiner *Renown FR246* was the second fishing vessel to come from McCrindle Shipbuilding Ltd of Ardrossan. Completed in 1987 she had a 671hp Deutz engine. Peterhead, *c.*1990.

Built in 1988 by J&G Forbes for the Watt family the 500hp *Assurance BF433* was a typical capacious below-16.5m Registered Length wooden-hulled single net and twin-rig trawler. Fraserburgh, 1990s.

Skipper Peter West fished with the 60ft 500hp twin-rig steel trawler *Golden West FR363* built in 1988 by James N. Miller & Sons. Fraserburgh, *c.*1990.

Staithes is situated on the rugged north Yorkshire coast. Early in the nineteenth century it was the most significant fishing port on the English east coast north of the Wash, owning some seventy to a hundred cobles and as many as seventeen larger Yorkshire luggers.

Fishing fell to a low ebb following the Second World War but better prices for fish and shellfish in the 1970s caused a small revival. At the start of the 1980s eight cobles and two open boats fished fulltime from Staithes. A view from Cowbar Nab, 1980s.

Right: The owner of the coble *Pilot Me* stored his fishing gear in this warehouse at Granary Yard in Staithes. 1980s.

Below: In an artist's house in Staithes the fireplace had tiles on which were painted the names of boats. 1980s.

Rebecca and *Our Lass* were the first medium-sized vessels from Parkol. The firm has built up a splendid reputation and by mid-2005 had produced a further eight steel boats in the just-below-15m to 19m size range for ports as far away as Stromness and Padstow. They included gill netters, scallop dredgers, crabbers and twin-rig trawlers. Whitby, 2000.

Opposite above: In 1999 Lockers Trawlers took delivery of the hefty and capacious 60ft twin-rig steel trawler *Rebecca WY790* from Parkol Marine Engineering. Skipper Michael Locker said 'She is a pleasure to go to sea in'. Whitby, 1999.

Opposite below: Built in 1957 by Gordon Clarkson in Whitby for Skipper David Peart, the 32ft 6in coble *Sea Harvest WY115* was beamier with fuller lines than earlier cobles. Whitby, 1990s.

The frightful carve-up of classic wooden vessels ground on remorselessly. In the dismal half-light of a January morning in 1996 I was among the little group of miserable people watching the trawler *Wakeful KY261* being cut up in Whitby. One onlooker remarked 'Poor old lass'. The 50ft cruiser-sterned vessel was built for Whitby owners in 1960 by James N. Miller & Sons.

Opposite above: In the 1980s and early 1990s, C. A. Goodall Boatbuilders at Sandsend was the principal coble builder in the Whitby area. Here, master boat builder, Tony Goodall (foreground), works on the 32ft 6in coble *Incentive WY373* ordered by Skipper Adrian Turnbull from Redcar. Sandsend, 1991–2.

Opposite below: Now based in Hartlepool, the 23ft coble *Bay Joe WY810* was built in Whitby in 2001 by two well known boat builders, Steve Cook and Lennie Oliver. Whitby, 2001.

Designed for purse seining and trawling for herring and mackerel, the 166ft *Vigilant PD365* and 189ft *Pathway PD165* were built during the 1990s by Simek A/S in Norway for the Lunar Fishing Co. of Peterhead. Peterhead, 2002.

Built by Hepworth Shipyard Ltd in 2000 the 78ft *Fairline PD325* (left) was the first new vessel of this size to be rigged as a seine netter for nearly ten years. Skipper John Buchan said 'Seine netting is environmentally friendly'. Peterhead, *c.*2003.

Above: Opened in 2001 the vessel repair yard and ship lift was an impressive development in Peterhead. Seen here leaving the building after a repaint, the 85ft twin–rig trawler *Arcturus LK59* was delivered from Coastal Marine Boatbuilders Ltd at Eyemouth in 2000 to Shetland skipper Bobby Sandison and his partners. Peterhead, 2003.

Right: Peterhead has continued its huge investment in fishing facilities. The new fish market, opened in 2001, is the most technically advanced in Europe and is designed to preserve fish quality at the market stage. Peterhead, *c.*2003.

Glossary and Notes

Perhaps there are those who look at these pictures but are new to the fishing industry and vessel design. The following glossary and notes may be of interest to them.

Fishing Methods

Trawl This fishing technique is used to catch bottom-swimming fish and employs a funnel-shaped net attached to the boat by two wire warps. As it is towed along the seabed it is kept open by floats and weights and otter boards.

Fly-dragging seine net This catches bottom-swimming fish such as cod, haddock and flatfish and uses a funnel-shaped net attached to the boat by long ropes. As the boat motors ahead, she hauls the ropes which converge and herd fish into the path of the net. In Danish anchor seining the ropes and net are hauled in by the vessel while she is lying at anchor.

Ring net A ring net is used to encircle herring shoals in sheltered waters and is worked by two boats.

Drift net At one time the drift net was the chief method of herring capture. Sheets of netting were joined end to end and hung vertically in the water in the path of on-coming fish, which were caught in the mesh by their gills.

Great lines These were lengths of thin rope with baited hooks attached at intervals. They caught large cod, ling, halibut and skate and were used by larger vessels fishing on rocky ground around Faroe, Iceland and Rockall. Long lines and small lines are lighter versions of great lines and are worked by inshore boats.

Pots and creels Pots and creels are baited traps which catch shellfish, chiefly crabs and lobsters. Laid along the seabed they are normally attached at intervals to a long rope.

Pair trawl Designed to fish at intermediate depths between the surface and seabed the pair trawl is towed by two boats positioned some distance apart.

Purse seine Purse seining basically involves setting a huge net in the form of an enormous deep bowl around a shoal of fish, such as herring or mackerel, swimming near the surface. The catch is brailed or pumped aboard the boat.

Other Things

Transom stern The after end of the boat ends square.

Decommissioning schemes These were designed to reduce boat numbers as a means of controlling over-fishing. British fishermen received payments in order to remove boats from the fleet, normally on condition that the vessels were totally destroyed.

English square-sterned cobles With their curious and complex shape, cobles are among the few traditional British working boats that have survived into the twenty-first century. Though primarily, beach boats designed for launch and recovery stern-to-shore through heavy breaking surf, cobles can also negotiate rollers or shallow turbulent water when entering or leaving unsheltered tidal harbours and creeks.

Nephrops Nephrops Norvegicus are popularly known as prawns. The tails are marketed as scampi.

Canoe stern The canoe stern is a sharp-ended counter which rakes aft at the centreline and has its fullest part at the top rail.

Power block This is a hydraulically powered roller for hauling nets.

Big five Herring pair trawlers could increase their catching capacity by working in groups. For example, some could be fishing while others were searching for more fish or were brailing their catches aboard.

Side-winder This is a popular name for a side-trawler, which tows both wires from one side of the boat.

Pocket trawler Pocket Trawlers were so-called to distinguish them from larger trawlers based at Aberdeen.

Motor fifies Having an almost vertical stem and stern, these were descended from the large Scottish double-ended sailing fifies and had a small wheelhouse. They had fuller lines aft to accommodate the engine.

Semi-bulbous bow A forward-projecting bulge at the forward end of the boat below the waterline.

Other titles published by Tempus

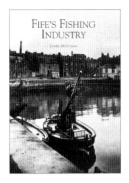

Fife's Fishing Industry
LINDA MCGOWAN

Linda McGowan charts the evolution of Fife's fishing industry through photographs from the Scottish Fisheries Museum, Anstruther. They concentrate on the East Neuk fishing villages that dominated Fife's fishing industry, showing the teeming harbours, the piers busy with herring lasses, and the shores piled high with baskets and boxes.

0 7524 2795 4

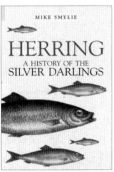

Herring A History of the silver darlings
MIKE SMYLIE

The history of the herring and those whose lives have revolved around taking it and getting it to the tables of the masses. The book looks at the effects of the herring on the people who caught them, the unique ways of life, the superstition of the fisher folk, their boats and the communities who lived for the silver darlings. For those who've neglected the silver darlings for lesser fish such as cod and haddock, there are numerous recipes to try.

0 7524 2988 4

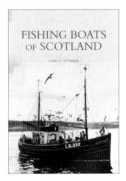

Fishing Boats of Scotland
JAMES A. POTTINGER

From Orkney and Shetland to the north-east coast, and from Fife to Berwick and around the west coast of Scotland, fishing boats have been an important part of Scottish maritime heritage. With a selection of 200 images accompanied by informative captions, this book vividly illustrates the vessels that played a part in the fishing industry in Scotland.

0 7524 3485 3

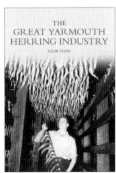

The Great Yarmouth Herring Industry
COLIN TOOKE

This lavishly illustrated and informative book describes the history of the herring industry of Yarmouth and Gorleston. Using over 200 archive images, many previously unpublished, Colin Tooke has compiled a vivid collection that records this hugely important aspect of Yarmouth life and industry. Many of the faces that worked in the industry over the years will be here and the experiences and hardships of working in such a demanding environment are also brought to life in this evocative volume.

0 7524 3760 7

If you are interested in purchasing other books published by Tempus, or in case you have difficulty finding any Tempus books in your local bookshop, you can also place orders directly through our website

www.tempus-publishing.com